Poetry from My Heart
A Journey through Feelings

Paul Guerin

Poetry from My Heart
Copyright © 2022 by Paul Guerin

All rights reserved. No part of this publication may be reproduced, distributed, or transmitted in any form or by any means, including photocopying, recording, or other electronic or mechanical methods, without the prior written permission of the author, except in the case of brief quotations embodied in critical reviews and certain other non-commercial uses permitted by copyright law.

Tellwell Talent
www.tellwell.ca

ISBN
978-0-2288-6566-7 (Hardcover)
978-0-2288-6565-0 (Paperback)
978-0-2288-6567-4 (eBook)

The Author

Paul Guerin was born in Castletownroche, a townland village in County Cork, in the Republic of Ireland. His early days were spent in and around Castletown where he came to love the countryside and was enchanted by the magic of the land.

As a young man, he lived in London, England and practiced as a chartered accountant. Later, he moved to Vancouver, British Columbia, Canada where he continued to practice his chosen profession.

Today, Paul lives in Surrey British Columbia, is married and has four children and four grandchildren.

Paul turned 75 in 2021 and this book of poetry, in part, is in celebration of this milestone and in part, is a legacy to his family and to his friends.

Paul still writes poetry as the inspiration comes to him and continues to work with a small number of clients, many of whom have become close friends.

Paul Guerin

Introduction

I have been writing poems throughout my life but until now I didn't think too much about it. I did little with them except store them away and occasionally read one or two. The interesting thing is that when I receive the inspiration to write a poem, it usually comes to me in a quiet place and the writing then flows easily and quickly. I prefer to write using a style of rhyming couplets which I learned and enjoyed when I studied English literature. Sometimes I wander from that discipline when my feelings override the limiting vocabulary available to the rhyming couplet style.

I am grateful for and humbled by this apparent gift, which I believe is universally inspired. Strangely, once I have written a poem, I usually forget what I wrote and when I read it again, I have little memory of where the original thoughts came from and it becomes a new experience. I can explain it by saying my poems are about feelings and when the particular feelings pass, so do their memories. For me, writing poetry is a cleansing process and for that I am thankful and because of that, I feel driven to share those beneficial results with others.

Shortly, I will turn 75 and I having been encouraged by family and friends to celebrate this milestone with this book of poems. For me, it is kind of a bucket list thing! It is more of a legacy to my family than anything else and I am glad finally to have the courage to bring my 75 years of thoughts and feelings to print.

I believe that the origin of these poems spring from my life experiences, without which none of these thoughts and feelings would have seen the light of day. It is important to me that the reader understands where these poems have come from and I hope that by sharing them, I can help others who may be struggling with emotional pain, to see their own truth and find the right path out of that proverbial emotional swamp.

My life has not been particularly easy. I experienced fear and great insecurity early on as a little boy in Ireland. Some enlightened souls say that we pick a difficult path in life so that we can experience pain and adversity, learn from our demons and then move on to do better things. Throughout my life, I have encountered many bumps in the road and from each of those "designer experiences", I have learned more and more about my feelings. Some of my lessons in life were painful but they were also an important part of my journey.

To balance the ledger, there have been many positive experiences also. For example, finding love, getting married, becoming a father, becoming a grandfather and many other amazing and fond memories that I have been fortunate to enjoy along the way.

To set the stage for the poems that follow, I will tell you a little about my journey to this point in my life.

As a very young boy, I lived in a small Irish townland village called Castletownroche. The village was situated in the very beautiful and pastoral County Cork. I had an Irish uncle who played in a showband and who taught me to fish at age four. I wrote a poem about that. My mother was absent and I never knew my father. I wrote another poem about that. We lived in abject poverty. I survived by the grace and loving kindness of an old Irish grandmother sporting a black dress, black shawl and a wicked temper driving a razor-sharp tongue. I called her Nana.

Nana taught me to fear [her] retribution and used it to keep me safe and provide security that I could find nowhere else. Well into my teens, my inner world was cast in fear and I had no real sense of belonging or attachment to anyone or to anything. The inability to handle those feelings, eventually led me to substance abuse. My journey along that road has generated much of the poetry of adversity, hope and inspiration that you will find in this book. I truly hope that those poems in particular, will salve the souls of those of you who are still trudging that happy road to destiny on your way back from hell.

Not surprisingly, I have had difficulty in maintaining healthy relationships throughout my life and much of the love poetry is about those failures and many, many, sorry attempts to return to love. Those painful/happy experiences had a major influence on my writing.

Anyway, that's enough to provide you with an idea of where my poems are coming from – the title of the book says it all – it's Poetry from My Heart.

Warmly,

Paul Guerin

Paul Guerin

Dedications and Acknowledgements

This book is dedicated to my wife Darlene who has always been there for me, very often at a cost to her own serenity. It is also dedicated to my children, Sean, Erin, Brigid and Haley and to my grandchildren, Liam, Olivia, Emma and Ariyah. I love you all dearly!

My thanks also go to all other family and friends who have been there, loved me and supported me along the years. I love you all and I am very grateful and humbled by all the support and the love you have given me. I am a lucky man!

I also wish to acknowledge my Mastermind partners, Bud Kanke, Patrick Cotter and Randy Purcell who have encouraged me to pursue my poetry and to share the results. You gave me the push and the courage to complete this work and bring the book to publication. Thank you, thank you, thank you!

Table of Contents

The Author v

Introduction vii

Dedications and Acknowledgements xi

Love Poems 1

Adversity 39

Solitude 87

Hope & Inspiration 123

Ireland [Éire] 177

Furry Friends 209

Epilogue 221

Love Poems

["For small creatures such as we, the vastness is bearable only through love." – Carl Sagan]

["You had me at 'hello'"
– Jerry Maguire]

["Sometimes I wonder if men and women really suit each other. Perhaps they should live next door and just visit now and then" – Katherine Hepburn]

Paul Guerin

YOU AWOKE MY WORLD

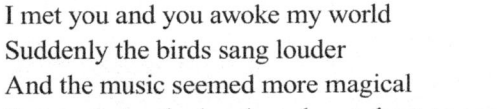

I met you and you awoke my world
Suddenly the birds sang louder
And the music seemed more magical
Our souls touched and our hearts beat as one

We both know that this is not possible
We will pinch each other to see if it is real
We both know there are hurdles ahead
But just now we do not care

I promise you I will never control you
Promise me you will love me always
Let us promise each other forever friendship
Let's become the best friends of our dreams

I promise you can be free with me
That I will always want you to fly on your own
I will always be here for you no matter what
I swear these promises to the God inside my soul

Time will pass and we will climb mountains
We are a team of simple, pure, amazing grace
The changes we have made in our lives are huge
Let's move forward with the speed of mutual lightening

Paul Guerin

At times I feel afraid of the pace and the risks this change may bring
At times I simply want to be alone to figure the right path
At times I stagger, falling and getting back up
Always, I have been there for you without a word

When you need space, it is freely yours to have
I will never hold you when you need to be free
My soul will never smother your free spirit
I will always hold you when you need to be held

Paul Guerin

A SWEET HALLO!

just a sweet hallow
to say that I love you so
I think you know
that the Universe
meant for us to be
together in love always

I know that we shall be
in heaven on earth every day
so great is our love and trust
and so great is our longing

I thank God for the gift
of our wonderful belonging

Paul Guerin

CONFLICTING PATHS

There are too many paths ahead
But can I choose only one
My feelings are confused by loyalty
I no longer know what is real
Something changed when I met you
But are those feelings real
If you are real what a gift that could be
I could keep you in my heart forever
I could love you forever
But I am too confused
Could we be together as loving souls
Are you really my soul mate
Why does reality block the way
Why can't I find the right path
Which way shall I go

Paul Guerin

LIKE EAGLES SOAR

You inspire my soul to reach the highest peaks
You light up the world I live in
With light so bright it dazzles and shines
Until all that is impossible becomes real

And the things I do are easier now because your love
Has made me strong and willing to risk
That which before I would have left untouched
And the results are amazing and stunning

I stand in awe and I laugh at myself
For ever doubting that I could not reach
For the highest peak and touch the stars
And find the apex of my soul

You have inspired the very best in me
To reach and seek my authentic self
To take a stand for what I believe in
To have the courage to trust in myself

And to believe that my dreams can come true
You have shown me how to fly with you
And to join with you with wings spread wide
Soaring into the sunset to meet the new dawn.

LET ME FLY ON MY OWN

She says:
I want to be free so let me fly on my own
I want to feel the wind in my hair and to feel it alone
To spread my wings and soar away
Through an azure dawn into a bright new day

So shiny and new just like that dawn
My soul will speak freely, heart to mind
Controlled no more, no longer a pawn
In the struggles of life, no longer so blind

Let me reach out now and touch the sky
Breathe fresh cool air on a free flight fall
Free as the gentle wind or a whispering sigh
Released with peace, no ties at all

Let me go now and spread my wings
And soar and soar I've things to do
To feel my soul, the truth to see
I need to know who I can be

Paul Guerin

He says:
I'll watch you fly my eagle friend
With winged fondness heavenly given
For I am sure that in the end
You will return by your love driven
Your heart, your soul, your body three
Will know that you and I are free

So fly away my eagle friend,
Spread those wings and fly away
Then some day, I know not when
You'll fly once more back here to stay

NOT THE MAN YOU NEED

I know your soul is hurting
I can feel it in my heart
I know I am the guilty one
Who failed you from the start

I know I disappointed you
I'm not the man you need
My ego whispered I was right
Your feelings not to heed

Instead of listening carefully
I tried to prove my case
I should have acted graciously
Not sought to win the race

I bullied you with words unkind
I drove your soul away
I tried and tried but couldn't find
The words to make you stay

In time there came that awful day
When you left me on my own
That was the price I had to pay
For driving you away from home

As souls apart now we must live
In quiet lonely places
Some loving kindness still to give
In separate safer spaces

Time and space will heal the soul
And drive away the pain
And when the half becomes the whole
We two can love again

My Love and I

My love and I are as one
We have bonded like crazy glue
We will never come undone
And every day we grow anew

My love and I are very sure
We trust each other like the air
Our love and trust provide the cure
We are both single and a pair

My love and I are happy souls
We are each other's special friend
The two of use make up the whole
We're sure our love will never end

There is no end to our embrace
There is no end to our mutual trust
There is no need to win the race
We have no fear we have no must

When I look into your eyes
I see your trust, I feel your heat
And my heart is filled with joy
Knowing we were meant to meet

Knowing you and your love
Has given me the gift of freedom
Has shown me that the power above
Provides us with both rhyme and reason

We are right together, you and I
There is no doubt we will succeed
And soar like eagles in the sky
For you and I are all we need

UNCONDITIONAL LOVE

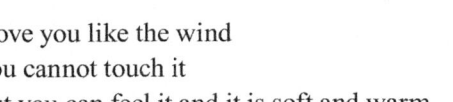

I love you like the wind
You cannot touch it
But you can feel it and it is soft and warm
It breathes in your face like a sleeping lover
And it touches you like a gentle breeze

I love you like the sun that burns so hot
And shines so bright and stands so high
But you cannot touch it
You can only feel the heat
That burns forever in me for you

I love you like the stars in the sky
Those stars that are untouchable
But are there to see all the time
You cannot touch the stars
But you know they will always be there

I love you like the swelling oceans
Those oceans that ebb and flood at will
Sometimes out of control but always there
You can surely touch the ocean
But its depth is beyond all understanding

I love you like the first blush of dawn
For the dawn is always there and rises early
And lasts throughout the day never fading
You cannot touch the dawn, but it is plain to see
Like the dawn, my love for you is always there

I love you like a newborn child so innocent and pure
For a newborn knows only that you bring it life
Never questions that you will always be there
Loves you unconditionally because it knows no other way
Because it trusts you with its life already

I love you like the rushing waters of the forest streams
Which flow so fast and strong and never stop
You can touch the forest streams and feel their strength
My love is as constant as the forest streams
And will flow forever to your womanly beauty
And touch you with magic hands of meandering longing

There is no measure of my love for you
It simply is there in timeless motion
It is without conditions without rules without boundaries
It will wrap you in its warmth forever and ask nothing in return
And it will endure forever because it knows no other way

My love has no conditions I simply love you
My trust is without question I simply trust you
My wanting you is endless I simply want you
I will take care of you always I just will
I will thank God every day for finding you

LAMENT OF A MAN

Woman I don't know who you are
But I see your beauty from afar
And I wonder if your soul is free
And if you might stay here with me

I think you know the things I need
To nurture me and help me breathe
With your support I can be free
I hope you will rest here with me

Woman you are a mystery
A gift to softly open
A soul that's captured history
With hearts so often broken

Woman I confess I'm lost
In turbulence my soul is tossed
Once I knew my hopes and dreams
But nothing now is what it seems

Woman please tell me how to act
So I can find the man in me
To bring me joy that I have lacked
Please love me now so I can see

Woman I beg you help me find
The confidence to keep me whole
The peace to ease my troubled mind
And love to save my inner soul.

Woman I wonder do you hear……..me….at all

CHOICES

If I choose to be a jerk
Then I am certainly a fool
If I choose to be a jerk
Then I am nothing but a tool

If I choose to be a jerk
No joy will I receive
Only pain without a perk
Loss of love and endless need

But if I choose to be a prince
In thought and word and deed
I'm sure to give you no offence
Just help to those who need

Now if I simply am a man
With kind and caring soul
I will find no "can't" in "can"
And there will be no "half" in "whole"

If I can heal my hurting soul
And share my love around
The half becomes the whole
And I'll stand on firmer ground

If I can stand in solitude
On a mountain in the sky
My thoughts of changing attitudes
Will help me find my "why?"

Why count the fears of younger days
Why court my insecurity
Why stay so lost in countless ways
Why live in immaturity

Why not be a mountain high
With room for all mankind
No jealous thoughts no bitter sigh
To sabotage an adult mind

Why not be in transformation
Helping other spirits grow
Filling them with inspiration
Bathing them in sunny glow

Why not let all fears transform
Creating love and pure insight
Why not heal a heart that's torn
And fill it up with pure delight

Paul Guerin

False Pride

It is quiet here in the room
And the house is at peace
And I wonder as I sit in tune
With the silence, will my longing ever cease

For a love that I can only dream about
But cannot reach because selfish pride
Snarls and shouts and shuts her out
Masking the kindness that cannot be

What good is it to yearn for another soul
If false pride struts its daily role
Playing its selfish drama, filling me
With rejection and its heavy toll

Of hurt and pain repeatedly
Arguing that I am right, that she will see
That I am a good and trusting friend
That will protect her in the end

Without real trust our eyes are blind
We cannot see the goodness here
Instead, we argue faults to find
Love is gone, we live in fear

And without love our heart is closed
And cannot hear each other's song
If we could only learn to see
That neither one is right or wrong

My best friend

Now my soul is awake and
My heart is open
I have come home to my best friend
I know that we are one
As our wings sweep the heavens together
And our hearts beat in unison
And our souls flow one to the other
Entwined for all eternity in love
In faith and in trust
I love you my friend
And you have set me free

Adversity

["Most of the important things in
the world have been accomplished
by people who have kept on trying
when there seemed to be no
hope at all" – Dale Carnegie]

["The ultimate measure of a man is
not where he stands in moments of
comfort and convenience, but where
he stands at times of challenge and
controversy." – Martin Luther King, Jr.]

["Storms make trees take deeper
roots – Dolly Parton"]

Paul Guerin

My Crumbling Wall

Feelings roll down like a rushing stream
Long trapped behind a crumbling wall
That held them there as in a dream
To hide where none could see at all

He didn't know where they came from
He didn't know he could speak out
He didn't know that they were wrong
He didn't know how loud to shout

Those hurtful words so long ago
Heard inside a mother's womb
Unwelcome child we hate you so
Those words heard loud inside that tomb

Years roll by and decades pass
Those feelings buried deep
Inside a room with walls held fast
A secret from the world to keep

Abandoned, feeling dead inside
A child devoid of love
His sad eyes one day opened wide
To see his true soul shine above

That day he felt so not alone
His soul was breaking free
He knew the wall was coming down
Authentic man for all to see

He felt the ancient crumbling stone
Crash down to free his soul
To let the man inside come home
To heal his heart and make him whole

WALLS OF SILENCE

I know that I hurt you, my heart was so cold
Chilled to my marrow with guilt within
I offered you trust with a promise so bold
You lowered your walls and let me step in

We had no fear, my promise seemed real
You told me you loved me, I smiled like a child
I felt ten feet tall, could finally feel
Like I hadn't before, those feelings were wild

Over time I frightened and pushed you away
I did what I promised I would never do
Your walls went back up one life-changing day
They'd never come down and I thought I'd lost you

But our love is not broken, we still have a chance
Hidden love is so strong, needing only romance
Those days that seem dark and devoid of all light
Can shine brighter and clearer more fully in sight

I feel present today, much stronger inside
With feelings for you I don't want to hide
Please, break out your smile instead of a stare
Look into me eyes, my heart is in there

I know I was wrong, there's no words I can say
I was angry and stubborn, I drove you away
Please trust me again and my promise to you
Is a life that is happy and a love that's still true

DREAMSCAPE

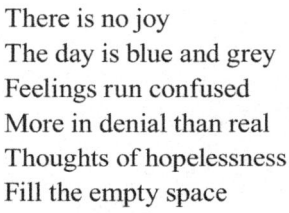

There is no joy
The day is blue and grey
Feelings run confused
More in denial than real
Thoughts of hopelessness
Fill the empty space
Heart is closed once more

What's left to do but rationalize
Maybe there is a chance
In shades of grey my eyes are closed
And I wonder what I fear

It's been a long time coming
And I contemplate an ending
Of all that I imagined
A dream that I just dreamed

Confusion lurks around
My thoughts run back in time
And I wonder where I'm going
Now my dream cannot be found

The mask will fall away
As authentic self appears
Attachments once so strong
Appear surreal and weak

Alone I am but not
I am the power of one
The universe is waiting
My journey's not yet done

Attachments are no more
I feel the power of one
The universe vibrates
A new song to be sung

WHY?

This way is all hard rock
Is the steep climb worth the try
I reach the crest as I take stock
And I ask myself – why?

If life is smooth and easy
Why is my mind so rough
Why must I feel uneasy
Why is my soul so tough

Why do I lack in faith and trust
Who shall I blame this time
Maybe, it's merely life's old rust
Causing my spinning mind to whine

Why, if all is calm outside
Does a storm rage through my mind
Why must my soul abide in there
Is there no safer place to find

Why?

DARK SHADOWS OF THE MIND

When the leaves in the trees vibrate in the breeze
As the sun drops down low in the sky
I remember those times when I felt ill at ease
Without knowing the reasons why

When the stars shine down and the moon glows bright
And the white clouds roll eerily by
I recall those dark times when nothing was right
Without knowing the reasons why

When darkness falls in the evening skies
And my mind mirrors black inside
I remember the past as my soul sadly sighs
Feeling wounds hiding deeply inside

Now I think of times past and my feelings reel
With thoughts of my troublesome mind
And I know that dark shadows are trying to steal
Any peacefulness that I can find

Those fears of the past don't want to let go
As those memories try hard to hold on
And they tell me again and again to say no
To the sounds of a happier song

So, I pray for some bright light to shine down on me
And I shout at those shadows to go
And I know that this bright light will set my soul free
And fill it with love, so my goodness can flow

Now the shadows are gone as I stand in the light
Pure shining divine energy
With a soft warm glow that will heal me tonight
And return great hope and well-being to me.

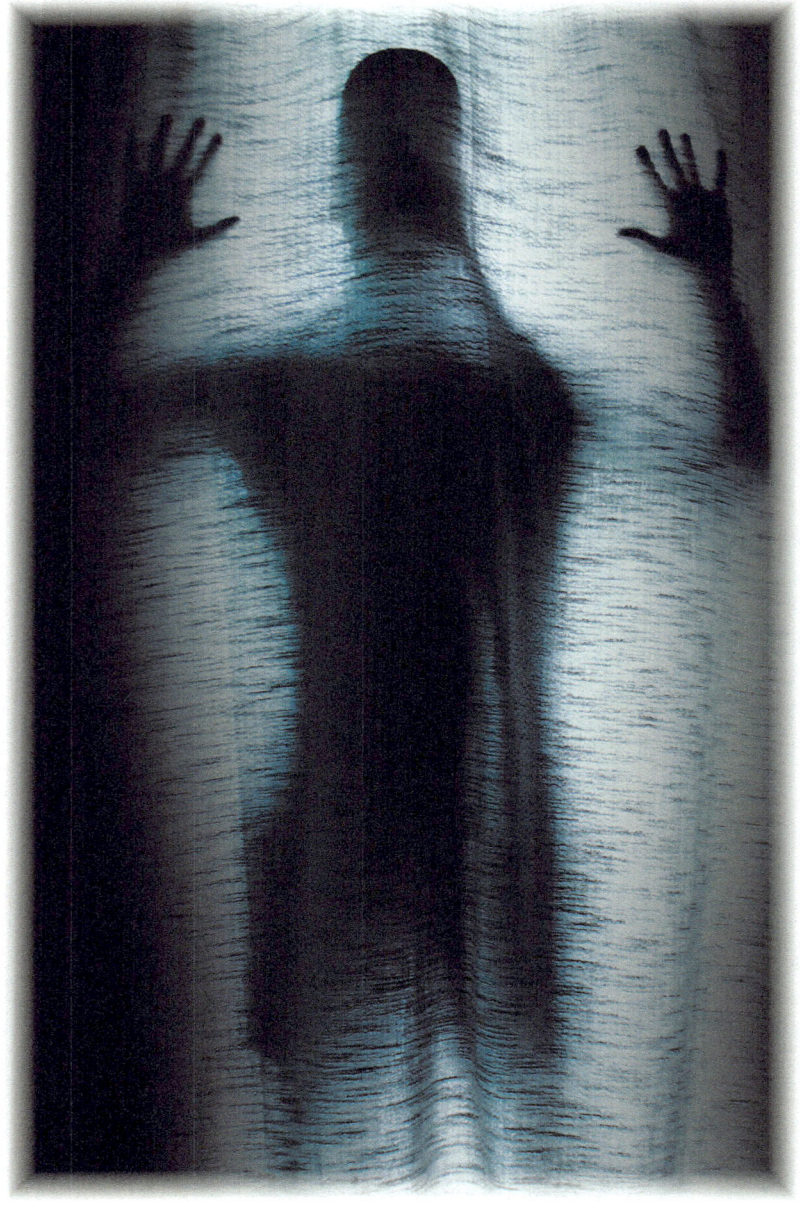

I FACE MY DEMON

I am alone as I face my demon
My heart and soul are in pain
I'm trapped, I've lost all reason
My thinking's becoming insane

I must find a way to recover
A way to be healthy and sane
I know that I need to discover
Why I'm standing out here in such pain

I'm alone as I face my demon
My inner Child's feeling so scared
I tell him I'll be there for him
Each minute to see how he's fared

So I push on again through the pain
Asking for help on the way
Whistling a frightened refrain
Please help me survive through this day

I need to find where I belong
As I seek out my higher power
By admitting that something is wrong
And asking for help hour by hour

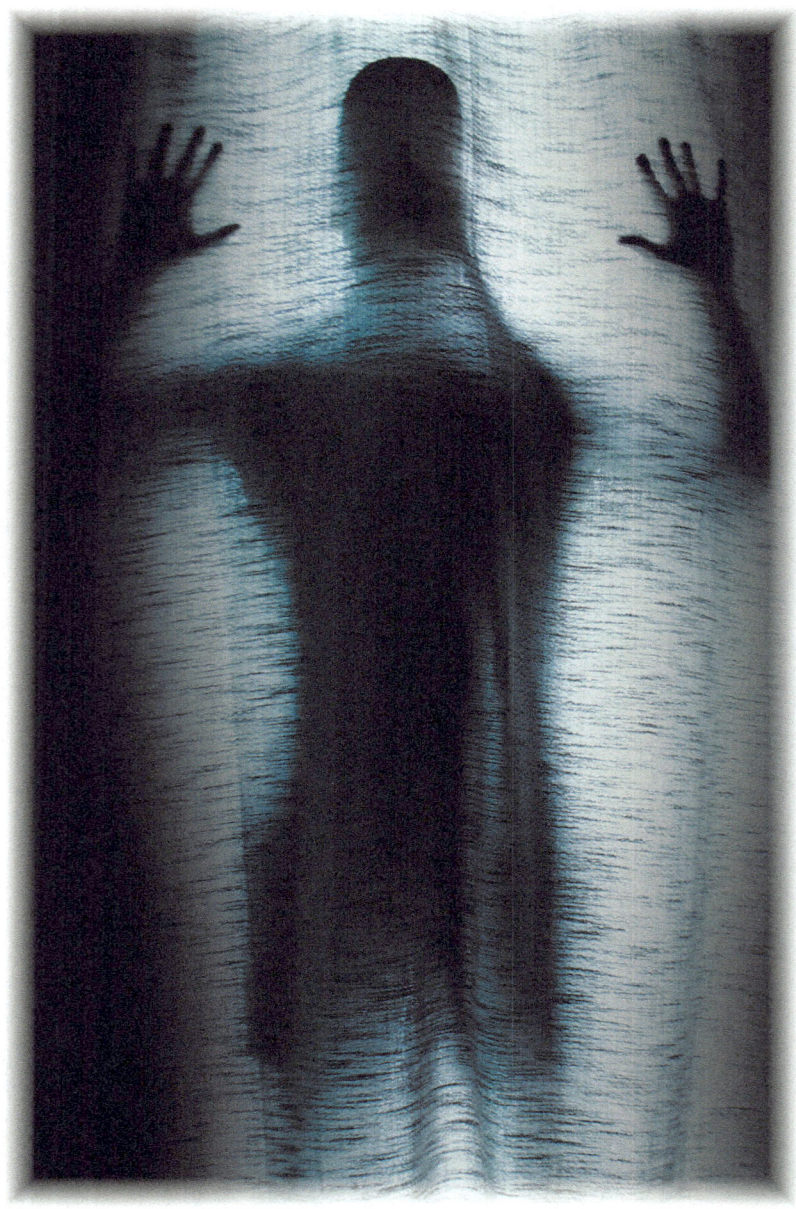

The demon returns with a cry
I must head him off at the door
And cast him aside or I'll die
Defeat him or I'll be no more

My conscience is calling out loud
Go redeem the boy-man, set him free
No more living in fear, no more shroud
Turn him into the man he can be

Epilogue

So roar foul demon, roar your worst
And I will scream loudly back
Today no quenching of your thirst
Today no further painting black

Tonight I'll break your crippling hold
Tonight my soul will be set free
And never again will I be told
To hide the light inside of me

Man behind the mask

I am in hiding behind a mask
A frightened poser, a *pretend me*
Trying to please reluctant souls
Whose friend I know I'll never be

I am safe behind the mask
Pondering over what to do
Being here is no easy task
I'm wondering if I'm one or two

I live in a shadow behind a mask
The real *I am* is hidden away
I say I'm fine to those who ask
But I'm just a fool in disarray

My life is full of doubts and fears
As I lurk behind a mask
Avoiding all who might judge me
I see no daylight in this task

I know some day when I have no fear
And I feel secure and whole
I'll share my truth for all to hear
And remove the mask to reveal my soul

My Soul Is Sore and Broken

My soul is sore and broken
And loneliness is here
With words that are unspoken
And a heart that's filled with fear

My life with you is fractured
The hurt, it comes and stays
But my heart is still enraptured
By your sometimes loving ways

This time I swore to make it work
Past mistakes to put behind
But still those demons hide and lurk
Inside my fractured, spinning mind

I know that we must surely try
To heal our troubled hearts
By doing so we'll see blue sky
The two of us must play our parts

If two will strive to make hearts whole
Two friends will walk away
With loving thoughts and strength of soul
To welcome in a better day

REACTIONS

What makes a man react is the question
The reasons are numerous we know
It may be a powerful suggestion
Or simply a partner saying no

For many years I was defensive
The reasons numerous we know
My inner thoughts were too intensive
My ego tried to steal the show

From an early age I felt alone
Abandoned child in motion slow
Dreaming of a special home
A quiet place where I could go

So I grew up afraid and lonely
Insecure and never whole
Feeling hurt and longing only
For a heart to fill my fractured soul

I looked to you to make me whole
To fix my childhood driven mess
I blamed you for my damaged soul
Abused and filled your days with stress

If I could have the time again
I would find a better path
With patient kindness I would win
The love sustained within your heart

It Takes Two

What good is life with no sunshine
What good is love when the spark burns out
What good is hope if there's no time
To see what living's all about

What good is talk if talk is all
What good are expectations false
What good is rushing for a fall
What good is missing life's true waltz

What good is love that won't give back
How shallow a dream that never wakes
How long can love last on a rack
Of hopeless longing and sad heart aches

How hard it is to take the pain
Of unrequited hopes and dreams
Of love that has no dual refrain
That flows as clear as mountain streams

For love takes two to make it real
Two souls to join like two souls can
And only then can two hearts feel
The joy when woman nurtures man

THE CLOAK OF LONELINESS

Tonight I wear a cloak of loneliness
The pit of my stomach feels hard and empty
I am numbed and I feel nothing
I am confused with nowhere to go

I am angry and afraid to feel
What I want most in the world is not here
I wait for nothing because I know it is gone
I am lonely, afraid and I hurt

I want to cry but what's the point
No-one is here to fix my breaking heart
As I sit here alone in my solitude
I wonder where I will go from here

I am tired of these feelings
What's gone is gone and I am here alone
I know that I should let it go, but I don't know how
There is only me and no one else to ask

I am lonely and I do not like it here
At least I will not be let down or hurt
I have had enough pain in my lifetime
And my heart and soul are broken - again

I am crying because the pain must go somewhere
And I pray that God will tell me what to do
As I sit here at my computer telling my tale
I feel like my soul is dead and I have moved on

This grief is for who?
Why am I so sad that I can't love anyone
What is the rhyme or reason of it all
God, please tell me what to do

My essence is screaming at me
And I sit here wondering, why me?
As I type I feel like some lost soul
Who has nowhere to go and nothing to see

What choice is there but carry on
Living one day or one minute at a time
And praying that God will make me strong
So that I will be whole some place down the line

As I sit here I think that I'm bigger than this
And I know that I'm strong for the ride
But I cannot see why my life has no bliss
So, perhaps it's not me but some demon inside

So I pray to be humble, to bury my ghost
And I hope that my call's loud and clear
My heart and my soul are dying inside
And I need, really need, to get right out of here

Young Boy

Young boy was frightened and lost
Father took off who knows where
Mother had left at emotional cost
Not leaving the love that a mother should share

Young Boy's life was strange and confusing
No security was coming his way
People were there, but not by their choosing
Young Boy felt sad by the end of each day

Young Boy was angry and too proud to cry
Finding safety in posturing hard
But really Young Boy was not getting by
Acting out as a bully in every school yard

Living in fear with thoughts barely whole
Feeling lonely outside of the clan
Young Boy embraced the need to control
His life as a leader of man

Young Boy's early years were hard to endure
No love, no security or hope
A young lad abandoned and so insecure
Denied of soft nurture, unable to cope

The years rolled by and Young Boy became
A man who could nurture his Child
And Young Boy gave up all notion of shame
Then Young Boy, the Man, came home from the wild

THE ROAD AHEAD

Your soul awoke and the road looked rough
You weren't sure where to roam
You knew your journey would be tough
A hard-fought struggle to make it home

It was hard to know which way to go
Which path was short or long
But along the way you came to know
Which choices would be right or wrong

Many came with troubled minds
With broken hearts to mend
And many journeyed on to find
The hopes on which they could depend

Like drowning souls who couldn't see
All washed up on the shore
Good souls who wanted to be free
Believing that there must be more

They walked along the rocky land
They journeyed to the end
And on that road they made their stand
And felt their souls begin to mend

They journeyed on, and on along
That long and winding road
They found the faith to keep them strong
To help them bear their heavy load

Those stony walls in proud array
Brought memories back to me
For I once travelled that same way
And found the truth that set me free

HOLD FAST

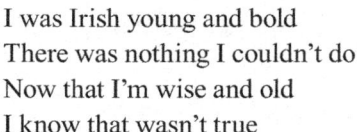

I was Irish young and bold
There was nothing I couldn't do
Now that I'm wise and old
I know that wasn't true

I held fast to a dream
In my journey through life
Until my dream became a scream
Filled with anger, fear and strife

As my dreams fell apart
And relationships died
Darkness entered my heart
Dressed as anger and pride

I had a need to be right
A compulsion to fix
Blinding my sight
Adding fear to the mix

The more that I tried
My life went to hell
The greater my pride
The further I fell

Holding fast to the past
Can't let go of the pain
This nightmare won't last
Take me out of the rain

Holding fast, I held fast
Protecting my pride
Justifying my past
Setting reason aside

The relationships cried
They couldn't survive
Inside tumult and shame
In the end they just died

It is no easy task
Letting go of the past
If I take off my mask
I won't need to hold fast

WITHOUT CALM WATERS

It is quiet here in the room
The house is at peace
And I wonder, as I sit in tune
With the silence, will my longing cease?

For a love that I can dream about
But cannot reach because selfish pride
Snarls and shouts and shuts it out,
Masking feelings we both hide

What good is it to be half whole
While false pride struts its daily dance
Playing its drama, filling my soul
With hopeless thoughts of dead romance

In hurt and pain, repeatedly
Arguing that I am right - you will see
That I am a good and trusting friend
Who will love and protect you to the end

Without calm waters our eyes are blind
And cannot see the goodness here
In hurt we shout words unrefined
That turn our love to hate and fear

If you can just forgive the past
Your open heart will hear my song
And you will have a love that lasts
And a man who loves you all life-long

DOWN HERE IN MY COCOON

It's deep down here in my cocoon
But the morning hour is here
I need to face the world real soon
Despite my nagging fear

I don't know why I feel this way
It's not authentic me
I need my angel strength today
I can't just hide to wait and see

The morning hour is early
And I am wide awake
The world outside is bustling
With its daily new intake

But now I must get out of bed
And face my fear head on
I'd rather stay down here instead
Even though that would be wrong

Faith will intervene I know
And drive away the fear
And if I ask to make it so
I know that faith will hear

And so I leave my safe cocoon
To face the world anew
I know the fear will leave me soon
Faith knows today there's lots to do

Solitude

["Knowing how to be solitary is central to the art of loving. When we can be alone, we can be with others without using them as a means of escape" - Anonymous]

["Solitude is painful when one is young, but delightful when one is more mature" - Albert Einstein]

["Nowhere can man find a quieter or more untroubled retreat than in his own soul" - Marcus Aurelius]

A QUIET MOMENT

A waterfall rushing down to the shore
Clear water lapping on the dock
The lake is saying more, more, more
May your torrent never stop

I sit on the boat tied up at the dock
It is quiet, no humans around
A slight breeze blowing makes the boat rock
And the wind makes a whispering sound

Birds are singing in the bush
With the roar of the water behind
It's so tranquil down here, there is no rush
To flash back to a fast-thinking mind

The sun is down behind the mountain now
As the sky turns red and then grey
Dog and human are walking the dock
No words are needed to say

We are grateful for such a safe hiding place
Where the cares of the world never stray
Where soul and heart find their own soft pace
And quiet is the noise of the day

A Spring evening

The humming of the birds
The trickle of the water
The sound of distant voices
Rising up in laughter

As twilight sounds entrance
The imaginative mind
And whirling little wings
Engage our highest senses

As fatigue merges with peace
We hear birds softly singing
Giving thanks for another day
Of safe and frantic winging

My senses feel the draw
As Nature shares with me
Her beauty and her strength
Of a perfect tranquil day

As dusk brings in the quiet
Mother Nature falls asleep
The sense of peace invades
My soul with love and hope

As darkness draws down
In solitude and stillness
I sit and contemplate a day
Of many new beginnings

The stillness of the evening
Brings clarity of mind
And gratitude for our homeland
Where we are safe and sound.

ABBEY BELLS

I sit in my humble room
In the abbey on the hill
Through the window I can see the moon
Shining in the night so still

From the church the sound of bells
Fill the air like mortar shells
Ringing, ringing their song so loud
Calling, calling their voices proud

Suddenly there is no sound
The bells have done their noisy poll
Silence returns and peace abounds
As I awake to the morning toll

It's peaceful here in abbey town
There is no rush to engage the world
It is a place of thoughts profound
Of wisdom and of joys unfurled

THE SOUNDS OF SILENCE

The silence cries out to me tonight
And I marvel my life is so slow
As the clocks tick away as though life just might
Drift onwards quietly with nowhere to go

I miss you tonight while we are apart
And my heart feels heavy and slow
I wait here for you so my life can restart
I drift in the silence with nowhere to go

And the silence cries out to me tonight
And the chimes of the clocks seem so sad
And I know that my soul will never feel right
When my heart and my mind are feeling this bad

I miss you tonight as I am quite alone
But I know that this pain I must feel
To grow in the silence a man coming home
With his heart and his soul that the silence will heal

And the silence cries out and the solitude screams
And the clocks keeping time tick on by
As I think of life passing and strange as it seems
In the silence I feel a young child's need to cry

I am lonely tonight and I pray that you care
I sit here with my heart full of fear
I'm alone in my soul with no hope left to share
And I'm dying inside with no one to hear

And the ticking grows louder and faster
And the chimes of the clocks sound like brass
And I know that these fears I must master
So I sit with these feelings and let the mood pass

And the silence blares out like a fanfare
Saying now it's the time to think hard
If you really are true, you'll know that I care
You'll stop living inside the other man's yard

I miss you tonight, you're the air that I breathe
And I dream that in time we'll be one
I think of the journey we're on and my need
For our souls to be joined and our day in the sun

Now the ticking draws down to a murmur
And the chimes of the clocks gently say
The night is so quiet with barely a whisper
And my heart and my mind drift softly away

I miss you tonight like a clock with no chime
As I dream of the sunny new day
I know that I'll need you like this for all time
And I know I will always love you this way

I feel solitude now and a silence serene
And the clocks sound like soft wind chimes
Now the night's not so lonely nor nearly so mean
As my heart with my soul start ticking in time

DARKNESS FALLS

Tick tock tick tock
The clock sounds loud tonight
As dusk falls in the cabin
We quickly lose our light

The frogs croak loudly in the woods
As the lake ripples down for the night
Ribbit they croak and say it is good
As for them the darkness is light

The ducks outside walk up and down
Looking for food on the trails
They know that the day is almost done
As they waddle and waggle their tails

The circling trout abound in the lake
As they merge in the ripples as one
Then they rise and jump creating a wake
Seeking the last of the sun

As night-time falls we embrace the dark
With lanterns of oil and propane
With an eerie ethereal click and a spark
We give light to a shadowy flame

We are grateful for all the gifts of today
For the goodness and joy we receive
And tonight it is easier for us to say
We have faith and the trust to believe

Paul Guerin

I AWAKE AT THE LAKE

I awake at the lake and the road I must take
Seems less narrow, less paved with surprise

The morning sunrise brings light to my eyes
As the shadows depart from the skies

The breeze blows so soft and so free
With its natural warmth and appeal

As hummingbirds hover round me
Bringing feelings of hope that are real

The morning awakes with its heavenly song
Singing everything's good, nothing is wrong

WATER ON THE LAKE

The water on the lake is quiet
As the evening light dims down
The candles flicker in the cabin
In the distance shine the lights from the town
The bell buoys blink red then green then red
As though saying it's time to rest now, rest now, rest now
The shadows of the forest head down to their dreams
Slipping slowly to the lake without a murmur
As night sets in and the daylight dies
The quietness of this place whispers, be still
The lake with tranquil darkness calls for peace
As the evening draws down
And the world sleeps

FORK IN THE ROAD

I sit here alone every night
Thinking how foolish I've been
Looking for further insight
For my future and what that will mean

Playing a dangerous game of control
Being needy and wanting so much
Wreaking havoc in a beautiful soul
Alienating all tender soft touch

I wonder if in time we will heal
Or whether too much damage is done
Is there anything left that we feel
Are there any more days in the sun

I sit here thinking alone
Wondering how the future will be
Will we be sharing our home
Or will we decide to be free.

LIFE ON THE LAKE

The sun shines brightly on the trees
Reflections of incandescent green
The birds chirp out soliloquies
Telling us how their day has been

All is calm in the forest terrain
Except for the buzzing of a bee
And the choir-like feathery refrain
Of life in the trees mere man cannot see

As water ripples on the lake
And boaters wind their journeys home
A gentle mist its shadows make
As mounds of mountains stand alone

The trees in mist and sky azure
Stand still with greenly silent might
Upon the mountain purpose pure
Observing evening's failing light

It's strange the evening feels so still
When the day is filled with throbbing life
As though the world has had its fill
Of daily living's pain and strife

As the sun goes down and shadows fall
Across the surface of the rippling lake
My thoughts of day begin to stall
With nothing further now at stake

Paul Guerin

Who am I?

I ask the question, who am I?
Am I my authentic self?
Who will I be when I die?
Will my soul sit on a shelf?

Or come again in body new
To nurture well a heart more true?

My leaning in my present life
Draws me towards the broken soul
Living life in pain and strife
My mission is to fix the hole

To lighten up the dark inside
Where shadows lurk and demons hide

To reach this goal I need to be
Myself in authenticity
And push the poser-actor out
Releasing fear, removing doubt

Once I feel me I start to see
The kind of man I need to be
A kind and caring loving soul
Compassionate and almost whole

Paul Guerin

So I start with me by setting free
My inner authenticity
Tell Ego no, don't run the show
I free my soul by letting go

Then I find it's really me
Waiting here to help me see

A COVID OUTLOOK

Looking at the mountain peaks
From cabin deck on high
Smokey grey cloudy streaks
Float planes in the sky

A busy cabin morning
Family all close by
Kids are busy storming
Parents loudly cry

Children's sounds of playing
Competing in all things
Mom and dad are saying
Be quiet my head rings

Cries of birds that sound so sweet
In green forest all around
And tall trees running down to meet
The lake on beachy ground

In the distance motors sound
Happy boaters on the lake
The cries of playing kids resound
With boundless joy to take

Post-Covid family magic
The long-awaited touch
Repairing what was tragic
Recovering our trust

Paul Guerin

The Covid years were hard
Hiding out in masks and fear
Hopes and dreams were marred
By things we couldn't hear

We lived in fear of something bad
We shut our dreams in tight
The things we heard just made us mad
We hid in darkness out of sight

Now our world is re-awakening
As our hopes and dreams renew
With big plans in the making
And lots of work to do

Its Hard to be a Butterfly

Is life an attempt at becoming someone I am not
To please someone for whom I am not the one
Trying to become the one that I am not
So that I can be seen and valued as Someone

My journey is hard, my vision distorted
I cannot see Me from the One I should be
Listening to others who don't see Me
As the man that I really am

If I choose not to be who I want to be
Hiding silently behind a mask
Faking good cheer while living in fear
The only one I am fooling is Me

To take off the mask and transform
I need to let go of what you think I am
And appear naked not giving a damn
Of outcomes I cannot control

When the time has come
I must transform as the One
That I really am without anger or guilt
Without remorse – I must be the I am

Paul Guerin

I PRACTICE THE PRESENCE...

I PPG throughout the day
Finding Presence in the Now
Spiritual practice is leading the way
To my essence and truth of the How

I practice the Presence all day
In each moment I find peace of mind
Loving kindness is also in play
To nurture my soul and quiet my mind

PPG is my daily routine
Keeping me centred and true
To the spiritual flow of life's stream
And an outlook that each hour is new

Hope & Inspiration

["You will face many defeats in your life, but never let yourself be defeated" – Maya Angelou]

["Impossible is for the unwilling." – John Keats]

["There is nothing in the universe that you cannot do or be if you are mentally ready." – Emmet Fox]

A LOVING TEACHER

In solitude far and away,
Pondering the meaning of life
I've thought of many things to say
To honour you to-day dear wife

When we met those years ago
Romance was "in the kiss"
Magic feelings fast to flow
Promising eternal bliss

But as the years went passing by
My problems came and grew
I came apart not knowing why
Or where my life was going to

The things I said along those years
Broke trust and hurt your heart
Words like darts brought doubts and fears
Hit home and drove our souls apart

Through all the heartaches you did not leave
Many times I thought you would
You showed me hope, made me believe
Grace and love could make things good

You showed me love was so much more
Than a churlish childish need
You helped me find that mystic shore
Where happy souls no longer grieve

You showed me that the soul within
Gave all the love we need
No cause to fight no war to win
Just loving words my heart should heed

You gave me space and let me go
With words of loving care
To a higher place where I could grow
And find my true soul resting there

Words can't express my thanks to you
For love throughout the years
The endless chance to start anew
Your help to find and tame my fears

So as I sit here calm today
I make this pledge to you
From this time forth I'll lead the way
And show you that our kiss was true

I love your soft and gentle voice
I love your easy grace
I think you were a heavenly choice
Sent here to guide me to this place

I love your happy pretty face
I love your angel smiles
I love you for the sacred space
You held for me along the miles

I'm grateful that you are my wife
I know that I lucked out
I promise you a better life
Peace, respect and free from doubt

A SHINY NEW DAY

I can see a shiny new light
Yes that light is shining on me
And it fills me with newer insight
And a view of what I can be

Now the dark of the past is behind me
And the future is calling to me
I embrace a new way of believing
As I journey to what I can be

And my senses are finally awakening
And my eyes and my ears grow alert
As I find the new pathway I'm taking
Far away from a terrible hurt.

For 'til now I was blinded by feeling
Only bad things and shades of the past
Now my body is no longer reeling
As I stand in the bright light at last

TEN ALREADY!

I can't believe you're ten already
The years have passed so fast and steady

You've grown so big and tall
Skilled with your soccer ball

Lacrosse is a great pick
You have a skillful stick

Your language skills are good
At times misunderstood

You love your sister always
You praise her for her good plays

You love your mom and dad
Even when they're mad

There is Grandma, Nana and Nona
And Poppa's always there too

The accolades are yours in dozens
You know we all love you!!

A SPECIAL FRIEND

You inspire my soul to reach the highest peaks
You light up the world I live in
With light so bright it dazzles and shines
Until all that is impossible becomes real

And the things I do are easier now because your love
Has made me strong and willing to risk
That which before I would have left untouched
And the results are amazing and stunning

Now I stand in awe and I laugh at myself
For ever doubting that I could not reach
For the highest peak and touch the stars
You have inspired the very best in me

You have inspired me to seek the apex of myself
To take a stand for what I believe in
To have the courage to trust in myself
And to believe that my dreams can come true

You have shown me how to fly with you
To join with you with wings spread wide
Soaring together into the sunset
Returning to meet the new dawn

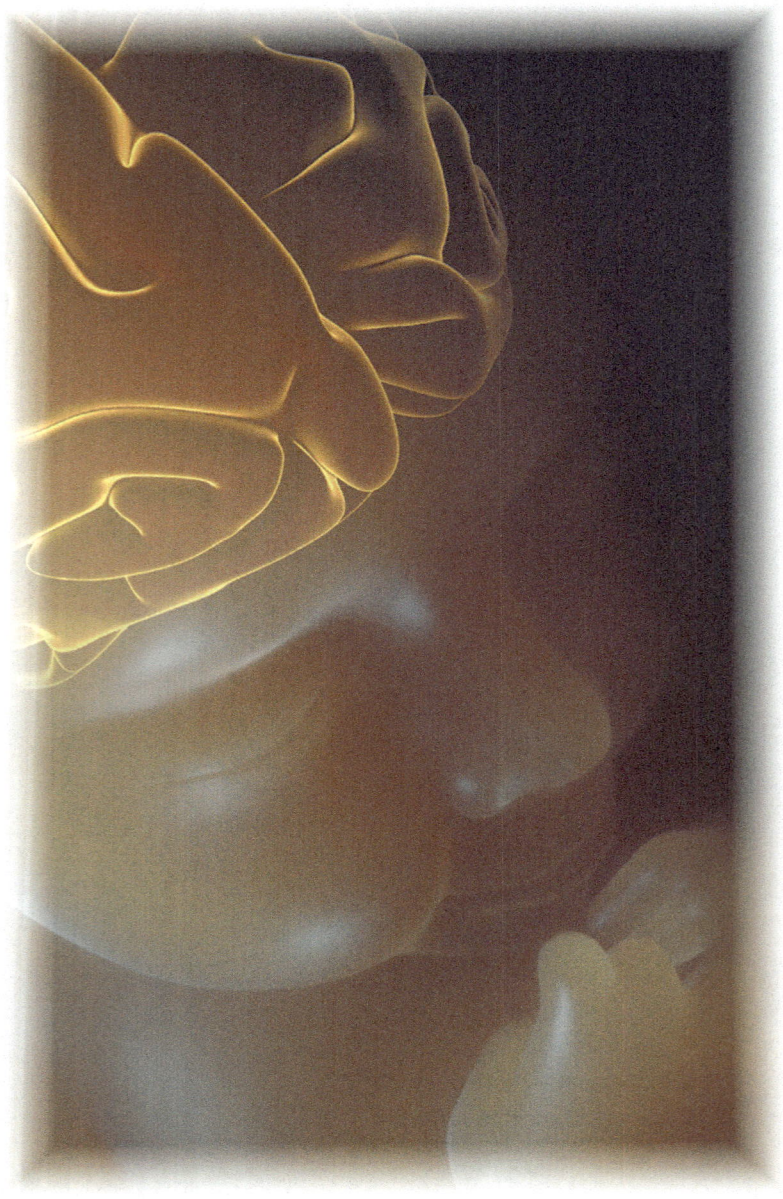

A QUIET MAN

I sit in a room with a quiet man
Talking of sad days gone by
Thinking could he be the one
To sing me a child's lullaby

Childhood days float through my mind
As I sit with this quiet man
And memories pour out, fast to unwind
As I start to find out who I am

Those lies years ago when I was newborn
Have taken a terrible toll
Delivered in sin, a target of scorn
Deep wounds to my baby soul

My arrival wasn't a happy surprise
Instead, I was greeted with fear
From inside the womb I heard angry cries
This new baby is not welcome here

I arrived on earth abandoned and scared
No mother or father in sight
To start my young life severely impaired
Devoid of affection and ready to fight

I grew up believing I did not belong
That alone I must struggle through life
Yet those years of adversity made me so strong
That my walls could not crumble no matter the strife

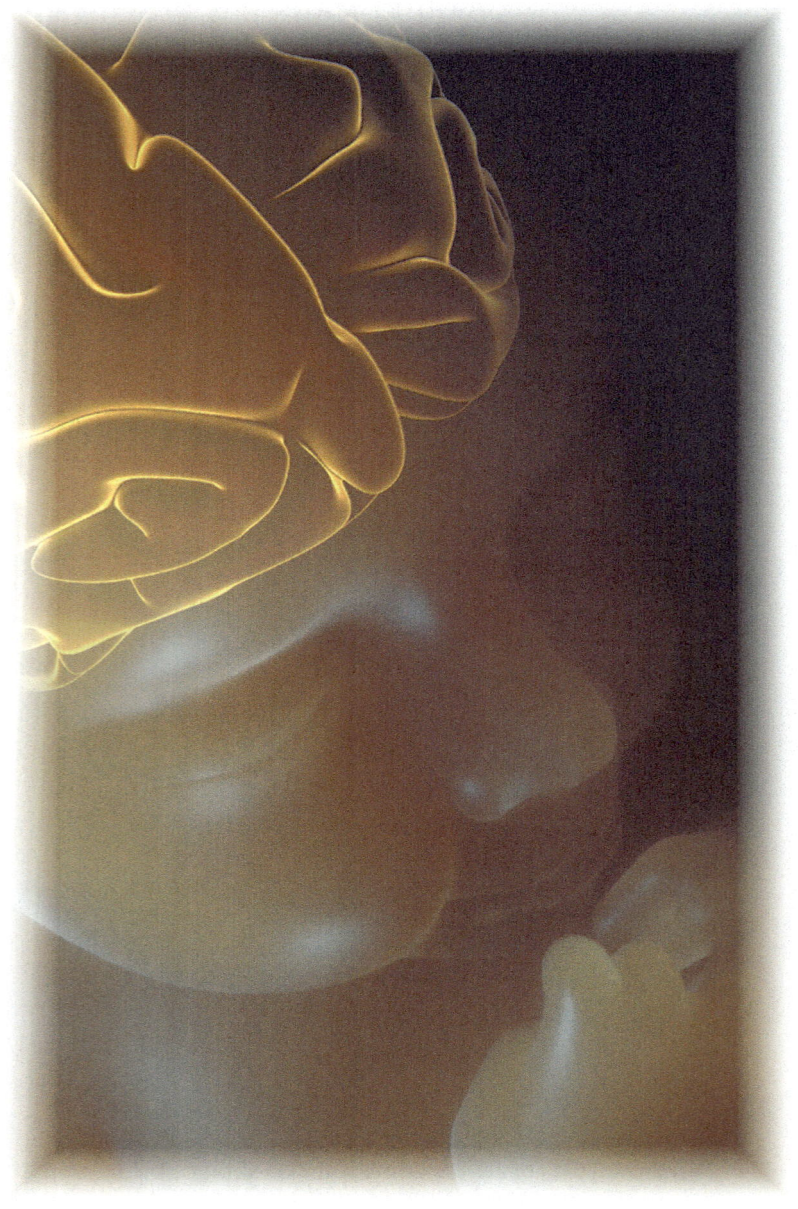

I thought I was 'less than' and worthless you see
I cared for no-one and hated myself
I thought that the world cared nothing for me
Sin-born and quickly put up on a shelf

The quiet man listens and strokes my sad soul
Then tells me what I need to do
He speaks incantations to spirits of old
He summons my soul group he hums a tattoo

This quiet man helps me to heal my hurt soul
With intuitive mystical might
He erases bad memories with a drum roll
He bows to my soul as it meets the bright light

How quiet is the man who holds spirit near
How calm is the water that shimmers with light
How blessed the soul that carries no fear
How cool is this man with unearthly insight

CHANGE I MUST

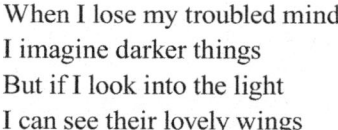

When I lose my troubled mind
I imagine darker things
But if I look into the light
I can see their lovely wings

What seems to be real is not
My mind rushes to a close
In my stomach there's a knot
Where comfort should repose

If my mouth obeys my mind
A torrent will erupt
Of words that are unkind
From origins corrupt

It is so hard to change
The dark feelings of my mind
They aim to rearrange
With voices unrefined

If I can change I must
It's a chance to win the day
It takes a magic thrust
To drive those shadows far away

When daylight reappears
A metamorphosis so bold
It drives away all fear
And let's the man unfold

Friendship

Written with a pen
Sealed with a kiss
Because you are my friend
I will send you this

Are we friends
Or are we not
You told me once
But I soon forgot

So I'll tell you now
And I'll tell you true
That I can say
I'm here for you

Of all the friends
I've ever met,
You're the one
I won't forget

And if I die
Before you do,
I'll go to heaven
And wait for you

I'll give the angels
Back my wings
And risk just payment
For my sins

To you I say
My friendship's true
My love and trust
I give to you

Shiny and New

I am shiny and new today
The very first day of my life
Now I know I'll be happy with you
For you make me feel worthy and right

You are shiny and new today
Your smile lights up the whole sky
You love me in a pure honest way
And together we'll learn how to fly

We are shiny and new today
And the future is sunny and bright
And the trust we have earned will not stray
Because it's so sacred and right

Some days have been long and hard
As thunder rolled over our skies
But the love that we share is not scarred
For each day I see light in your eyes

I'm amazed at the strength of our love
And the bond that we feel as a pair
And I know there's a strength from above
Looking out for this cool love affair

And I stare at the love in your eyes
As you tell me you love me this way
And I know we're a shiny surprise
In the dawn of a shiny new day

And today we are shiny and new
And we love this first day of our birth
Now we'll live not as one but as two
Finding freedom and joy in laughter and mirth

Paul Guerin

JOURNEY ON

When the path you're on is so unclear
And your feet move stone by stone
Just trust your faith will calm your fear
And help your soul to find its home

When fear is always telling you
Don't bother, you can't do it
Trust that faith will see you through
Wake up and move right to it

Just take your courage by the hand
And walk the walk my friend
And know that hope will see you land
On sunny shores around the bend

Your journey will go on and on
Your search will have no end
But faith and trust will keep you strong
And help your wounded soul to mend

These feelings I must share with you
Wise words from friend to friend
For I have travelled this road too
And know there's hope around the bend

Paul Guerin

Remember that your bond is strong
With soulmates tough and kind
From old times past and lives long gone
They'll mould the workings of your mind

They'll tell you that your light will shine
Just like the morning sun
They'll promise you a better time
With boundless joy for years to come

Just think how far you've come my friend
Your hopes and dreams came true
With faith and trust there is no end
Of peaceful days ahead for you

THE WORDS YOU NEED TO HEAR

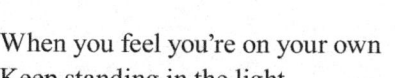

When you feel you're on your own
Keep standing in the light
Soon you'll find your not alone
And better times will be in sight

It's hard to know what you should do
When nothing much seems right
Know that faith will help you through
And ease the darkness of the night

With courage you can find your way
Through the many trials of life
To find a place where you can stay
Safe from fear and free of strife

Your journey will be hard and long
On that you can depend
But love and hope will keep you strong
And faith your wounded heart will mend

Heed these words I offer you
To send you on your way
For I have travelled this road too
And know the price you have to pay

A wounded soul is hard to mend
When burdened down with fear
But if you journey to the end
You'll find the words you need to hear

THE MORNING HOUR IS EARLY

The morning hour is early
And I am just awake
The world outside moves barely
With the morning's new intake

Feelings of fatigue run through me
Yet I am grateful for my life
And the good things that renew me
For the kindness of my wife

I think about my children
And I thank my God for them
For my beautiful grandchildren
For their grace that comes from Him

I think about the years gone by
Of the suffering, fear and strife
When my faith in God like some bright sky
Shone through the darkness of my life

I think about the lessons learned
Of the struggles getting there
And the way my heart and soul has yearned
For loving dreams, with friends to share

And I know that I am safe today
That my soul can rest in peace
And happiness has come to stay
My faith in God shall never cease

The morning hour is early
Now I am wide awake
The world outside moves barely
With nothing more at stake

Paul Guerin

SHINY SHIMMERING WATER

Shiny shimmering water, a reflection of the sky
With mist that hangs so low and white
So gentle to the eye at night
Above the lake so softly, drifts by with a sigh

The moon shines down in white array
Its shadow shimmers in the lake
Its beaconing hand says come here, stay
With me forever, your life I'll take

The stars shine bright in a darkened sky
Their shadows glisten in the lake
They speak to me and ask me why
My hapless life I need to take

Then hope shines down into the lake
With misty fingers, shimmering bright
And says my life I should not take
And tells me, quick, look to the light

Tonight the lake will save my soul
With rippling hope in waves that break
Upon its shores it takes no toll
Of hapless souls, no lives at stake

Shiny shimmering water a reflection of the sky
With mist that hangs so low and white
So gentle to the eye at night
Above the lake so softly, drifts serenely by

THE GUARDIANS

My life is like a garbage can
I really wonder who I am
Am I recycled or quite new
Am I a single or maybe two
Or am I many in a row
Filled with rubbish set to go
Am I waiting for a ride
Or simply letting my life slide
Are my smaller smelly friends
And their sacks an older trend
It seems we're objects in a row
Without another place to go
Full of stresses and life's strains
We're the guardians of what remains

Thanks Mate

What a friend you are
The greatest mate by far
The best a man could find
A heart and soul so kind
That it belies measure
You really are a treasure
I've come to love you dearly
You helped me to see clearly
That I have many choices
That others with loud voices
Are there to help me see
That I am fine with me

Thanks mate!

MUTUAL TRUST

Trust in me and I'll trust in you
It's quite an easy thing to do
When I think what you mean to me
And I think what I mean to you

Two souls meet in heavenly flight
Divinely present and inspired
Two hearts merge and know it's right
Their trust will burn forever fired

As time goes by trust gets impaired
By life-long hurt and pain
And memories of being scared
Standing in the freezing rain

If souls are strong and hearts entwine
Trust will surely build and grow
And all it takes is the hands of time
To know our soulmate will not go

As time goes by trust will be there
And hearts will start to heal
And we can share then as a pair
Of soulmates not afraid to feel

Trust in me and I'll trust in you
And together the better we'll be
With a kind word here and a soft touch too
We'll travel through life happy and free

When times are tough and the going's rough
Our souls must work hard to be free
With trust in our hearts, it won't be that tough
To stand in the light so that we can see

My Darkened Moon

The pain I carry is so intense
It has no rhyme or reason, it makes no sense
It comes and goes like a lunar cloud
And buries all goodness in a shroud

At times like these I feel alone
There is no-one to share my load
The moon once bright, appears now stone
As I stare at a dark and empty road

My shadow-self is the darkened moon
An angry ego engaged out there
While judgements fill the awful gloom
My soul cries out in dark despair

Move to the light my soul cries to me
Look up and find your power within
The pain you carry will set you free
It has no substance, its logic's thin

Look hard and find the power to choose
Light over darkness, peace over pain
Look harder and feel the light infuse
Your heart and soul with love again.

No Platitude

I am full of gratitude
In that I have no latitude
It's certainly no platitude
To say I love this attitude

Today the sun was shining
Its warmth had perfect timing
It brought a silver lining
Our love and hope defining

To-night the stars are sparkling
In the sky so dark and startling
And the moon is shining brightly
As the day winds down politely

So, I am full of gratitude
And yes, that is no platitude
I need to keep this attitude
In that I have no latitude

OUR ADVANCE

Sitting by the airtight stove
In the cabin on the lake
Thinking of a treasure trove
Of promises to make

We're here together to "advance"
And clear our busy minds
To bare our souls, our lives enhance
With spiritual thoughts still undefined

We take a vow to not complain
And promise we shall listen
We shall not judge or give advice
We'll allow our souls to glisten

As we sit and watch the lake
We're filled with gratitude
We know that love is what it takes
And in that there is no latitude

We celebrate the here and now
We live right in the moment
We don't ask why, we do ask how
To transform and make atonement

We conclude that gossiping is sad
It hurts our happy souls
Judging others is also bad
And robs us of our daily goals

Resistance is a hurtful thing
Acceptance is the way
An open heart will surely bring
Peace and joy to fill our day

Letting go of petty thought
Requires immediate action
We recalled all the times we fought
With zero satisfaction

Sitting here in our Advance
Looking at the lake
The trust we build helps to enhance
The spiritual path we choose to take

We are so grateful for our brothers
In the cabin on the lake
This quiet place helps us discover
All the steps we need to take

A HELPING HAND

As the sun promises a bright new day
My heart beats loudly in its space
And I think how we can find a way
To make the world a better place

Can we cause the world to change
By being kind to one another
Should our goals be rearranged
To help a sister or a brother

If we help someone today
Will that assist the world to heal
If we follow the mystic way
Will our lives become more real

If we practice loving kindness
Will that help the world to see
If we look to faith, not blindness
Will that help us all to be

Ireland [Éire]

["These things, I warmly wish for you - someone to love, some work to do, a bit o' sun, a bit o' cheer. And a guardian angel always near" - Irish saying]

["We Irish are too poetical to be poets; we are a nation of brilliant failures, but we are the greatest talkers since the Greeks" - Oscar Wilde]

["May your day be touched by a bit of Irish luck, brightened by a song in your heart and warmed by the smiles of the people you love"- Irish Saying]

RELIVING THE AULD SOD

Ireland bound I am again
Flying through the wind and rain
The emerald isle is calling me
To relive childhood history

The sun is shining bright and clear
As steadily I make my way
To Dingle Town two hours from here
Where land and sea combine to play

What is it that attracts me here
To the land where spirits run so free
Where dogs and sheep in harmony
Run wild for all the world to see.

My childhood roots are calling me
Their soulful echoes from long ago
Invade my happy memories
And fill my dreams with thoughts to go

To this land that nurtures me
And heals my scars from bygone days
Fixing broken memories
And helping me in countless ways

When I am here I feel at home
The people smile and welcome me
And as across the land I roam
I feel its magic set me free

O magic land of mystic green
I cherish you with beating heart
As I walk among your hillside streams
I know that we shall never part

Paul Guerin

A SAFE QUIET PLACE

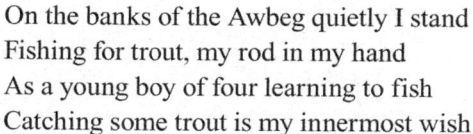

On the banks of the Awbeg quietly I stand
Fishing for trout, my rod in my hand
As a young boy of four learning to fish
Catching some trout is my innermost wish

I'm in Castletownroche, Republic of Éire
The Emerald Isle and land of the faerie
Near the city of Cork in its namesake county
A fresh green land of pastoral bounty

A few of my family members are near
I'm alone in my soul and my heart's full of fear
No mother is there to nurture or hold me
No loving kind words, no arms to enfold me

I grew up feeling far less than secure
Posturing toughness but always unsure
Seeking the nurturing a young boy had missed
Determined to always stay high on the list

I will never forget those old Irish days
A young child abandoned, fear running on high
Trying to explain in so many ways
Why I felt so unsafe, why I hurt, why I cry

Forsaken I was but I no longer am
And now I can nurture the boy in the man
I know that a young lad of three had no fault
And now that it's time for the man to cry halt

I'll suffer no more with the shame and the guilt
I'll embrace and enjoy the great life I've built
I'm a young boy no more, no reason to blame
I will trust who I am and let go of this pain

I will move on with life in the best way I can
Never forgetting that now I'm a man
I can fend for myself and nurture my soul
And fix past neglect and make myself whole

But I'll always remember those times at the river
As silky black waters rushed down to deliver
Solace to me and the men as we fished
As evening drew down with a murmuring wish

In those special brief moments, I didn't feel sad
Nothing could hurt me or make me feel bad
Life was a babble of silvery water
With nothing to change and nothing to alter

Down by the Awbeg, the men all around
Standing there quietly, not even a sound
I'll never forget their murmuring voices
As evening drew down and flies were their choices

I'll always remember the black and still water
That's there to this day, never to falter
The reeds and the rocks surrounded by cow pies
The cliff and the trees reaching up to the low skies

All my life I've held on to the magic back then
And I'll never forget those old fishermen
Who loved me and helped me feel safe and feel free
As they murmured and murmured their souls out to me

THE FAERIE RING

When I was a young boy of three
A Faerie Ring appeared to me
Down at the bottom of a hill
Danced little souls with lots of will

For years I thought I dreamed of this
Those little elves so full of bliss
Dancing in a Faerie Ring
It really was a magic thing

They say that Faerie Rings appear
To certain souls whose paths are clear
So loving are these apparitions
They come to us without conditions

To this little boy of three
They looked so special and so free
That he remembered them through life
Throughout all troubles and all strife

Then one clear day he came to see
Their gift to him was meant to be
He learned that Faerie Rings appear
To those alone who live in fear

And now he knows that this was good
And means his fear was understood
For Faeries don't appear to those
Who can't defeat their fears or foes

So, if you see a Faery Ring
Enjoy this very special thing
And know it just appeared to you
To show you what you need to do

FEEDING A HUNGRY SOUL

Standing on a mountain looking at the sun
The world seems so small and distant
Thinking of the person I have become
Authentic soul, true and non-resistant

The mountain air is damp and cold
Caressing my inner senses
With hands so soft and lips so bold
Driving through my hard defenses

Looking down from high above
The drama unfolding before my eyes
My only thoughts are kindness and love
As sunshine fills the bright blue skies

Holding space for those in need
Is my new-found daily task
Kindness compassion and love to feed
Hungry souls too hurt to ask

A kind word here a soft smile there
Will heal a hurting soul
A loving word, a show of care
Will mend what's broken and make it whole

FISHING IN AN IRISH EDDY

The fish...

The fish swam up the mountain stream
Close to bottom under hanging trees
Seeking a place to hide and preen
In tranquil waters and be at ease

It has a place to reach today
Where spawning sisters softly lay
On sandy bottoms in quiet waters
Spawning minnow sons and daughters

The sun now shining on the stream
Sends sparkles down the rippling run
The fish lays there as in a dream
Basking in the warming Sun

The fisherman....

A shadow draws across the stream
Spreading o'er the fish so still
A fisherman who has a scheme
To hook the fish and make his kill

The fly cast....

Fly and line hit water hard
Mother fish makes not a move
Today she holds a winning card
Her focus sound, no more to prove

Missed again....

Fly hits water like sprinkling rain
The fish darts nimbly to midstream
Fly reaches out too late again
And the fish turns fast and heads upstream

The moral....

Fishing's not catching we are told
But another moral is learned here
Make sure your fly cast's not too bold
Or your fish will swim away in fear

Down on Inch Strand

The sun was shining on the Strand
The white tipped mountains touched sky of blue
As miles and miles of golden sand
Ran on and on beyond our view

The surf crashed on the endless sand
Shimmering water tipped in white
The hills around the horseshoe Strand
Looked down with green unspoken might

The breeze blew steady from the West
Landing on the sun-drenched shore
The mighty ocean took no rest
Returning to this land of yore

The sun was warm and the winter breeze
Caressed us on the shore
The waves crashed in with powerful ease
Returning to this land once more

A RAINY IRISH MORNING

I look out the window and I see the rain
In this cold windy February morn
The rain is wet but I feel no pain
As I sit here admiring the Winter storm

It's cold in the kitchen but the coffee is hot
I hear the washing machine grinding a load
And I think about the future and our human lot
And of what to expect as I travel this road

So I sit here in the land of the Faerie
Safe among hills soft and green
That fall and rush to the rolling sea
Whispering promise of good things unseen

Feelings of goodness vibrate in this land
Brightening its green hills and dales
Reflections of loving soft gentle hands
Shining out goodness for this land that prevails

I sit here and ponder then the sunshine appears
Through the storm and the wind and the rain
Bringing bright light to the rain and its tears
And hope for mankind to be free from its pain

And goodness vibrates throughout this land…..

Paul Guerin

THE KING OF CONNOR PASS

A sheep gazes through the mountain mist
Seeking a softer landing
A lake in the distance he can't resist
A place for better standing

He stands on moist and mossy slope
A sentinel with a mission
His horned head looks down the slope
For a sunnier safe position

On Connor Pass the grey rocks gleam
And mossy grass lines ragged hills
Grey skies look down on mountain streams
As grazing Sheep his belly fills

In this wild and rocky place
Green windy mountain scene
King Sheep strolls at a tranquil pace
Grazing softly as in a dream

On Connor Pass King Sheep stands tall
A sentinel black and white
Gazing down he sees it all
A world of mist and mottled light.

THE NARROW ROADS IN DINGLE COUNTRY

Narrow roads wind to the Strand
Seeking out the ocean
Rolling hills embrace the land
Like poetry in motion

Grey rock walls like nature's hand
Hold sheep and pasture in
Grazing rams with thick head bands
Look on and chew with knowing grins

Little towns with Gaelic names
Are dotted here and there
Pedal bikes on narrow lanes
Heading out we know not where

Bright blue skies with clouds pure white
Move with silent grace
Shimmering seas complete the rite
Of passage in this peaceful place

Paul Guerin

TRAVELLING HOME

Travelling home from Dingle, the rain starts to fall
But the hills are still emerald green and the stone walls grey
As I drive along the narrow roads I feel the country's call
Come back, come back here, we want you to stay

With some feelings of loss I want to go home
But my ties to this land are hard to break
There's no place like this wherever I roam
No better place for my Spirit to awake

I arrive at Cork airport and the rain is coming fast
As if to say, see, the sun has gone to sleep
Inside I feel dejected to leave my distant past
But my soul has found a lot of things to keep

In prayer and meditation, I spend my last night here
And thoughts of green hills and stone walls invade my mind
My heart is sad and I have some lingering fear
Of going home and what my heart will find

Now I sit in the airport awaiting the plane
Thinking of going back home
Knowing that to fear is simply insane
When there's peace and serenity wherever I roam

Fear is Not Real

I have no fear of flying
Flying will be fun
I am not scared of dying
My life is not yet done

Fear is not good thinking
The thoughts are never real
The concept's really stinking
The images surreal

False **E**vidence **A**ppearing **R**eal
Is what fear wants to be
It doesn't care how bad you feel
It hopes the truth you will not see

Put an angel on your shoulder
And a guardian at your gate
Then your Spirit will be bolder
And fear will hesitate

And read this poem every day
So fear will disappear
Because we know fear will not stay
When healthy thoughts are living here

Furry Friends

["The only creatures that are evolved enough to convey pure love are dogs and infants." – Johnny Depp]

["If there are no dogs in Heaven, then when I die I want to go where they went." – Will Rogers]

["There is sorrow enough in the natural way from men and women to fill our day; but when we are certain of sorrow in store, why do we always arrange for more? Brothers and Sisters, I bid you beware of giving your heart to a dog to tear." — Rudyard Kipling]

Paul Guerin

MURPHY BOY

We had a dog called Murphy
And he was quite the pup
He looked at us with deep dark eyes
As if to say "what's up"

His look was quite traditional
His heart was strong and true
His love was unconditional
His look said "I love you"

He really loved his mistress more
Although he loved me too
He liked to lie flat on the floor
With nothing much to do

He loved to cuddle like a cat
High on your shoulder too
He liked to lie down on his mat
With nothing much to do

He loved his walks and cookie treats
He didn't like the rain
He was most happy when he'd eat
And snored with loud refrain

We loved our Murphy boy a lot
He was so loyal and true
He brought us joy right on the spot
He told us "I love you!"

Thanks Murph! In our hearts forever!

Paul Guerin

Brody Boy

Brody was so tough
He started life real rough
Thrown in a puppy mill
Where he didn't get his fill

No loving and no food
His treatment was so crude
But now he feels so good
Lives in a better 'hood

Around one o'clock each day
He comes around to say
Hey mister, give me food
In a manner not so rude

Brody was so tough
But nowadays not so rough

Best Friends

Murphy and Brody were Shih tzu twins
They had long shaggy ears
They were the most amazing friends
So loyal throughout the years

They were our friends for many years
Sharing licks and loving ways
Now they're gone we're full of tears
They can no longer share our days

Murphy was a cat-like pup
He'd bow his head and purr
Brody liked to stare at us
Saying, food or I won't stir

Murphy had a light brown coat
Brody's was snow white
Murphy liked to bark at night
Brody liked to fight

Murphy ate his food too fast
Brody ate his slow
Murphy liked to run and play
And Brody loved that so

They were happy brothers two
Playing games galore
They'd run and bark and wrestle
And fall down on the floor

One day when Murphy could not walk
We had to let him go
We were so sad we couldn't talk
Since then we've missed him so

Four months after Murphy died
Brody left us too
We said goodbye, we cried and cried
As his eyes said I love you

They were two most loyal friends
And we had to let them go
They went to sleep no painful end
Because we loved them so

They're both in doggie heaven now
With lots of food we know
They'll be waiting for us there
Because they love us so

Farewell Brody Boy

We hear your footsteps walking
Across the wooden floor
Tomorrow we won't hear them
You won't be here anymore

You were a quiet loyal friend
Your presence always there
So sad to think this is the end
Of the time we have to share

Its hard and hurts to see you go
But we know it's for the best
Your tired old body is running slow
Now it's time for you to rest

A dog is such a special friend
Trusting loyal and true
No matter what, in the end
He's always there for you

We love you Brody boy!
We will always miss you!

Epilogue

["Poetry – a literary work in which special intensity is given to the expression of feelings and ideas by the use of distinctive style and rhythm."]

["Poetry - writing that formulates a concentrated imaginative awareness of experience in language chosen and arranged to create a specific emotional response through meaning, sound, and rhythm."]

Poetry means different things to different people. For me, it is all about feelings. If it captures the emotions of the reader, a poem will resonate and fill the soul. It can mean everything to one person and not much at all to another. The mood of the reader and no-one else, determines the outcome. For example, love poems are wonderful when you are in love and their passion is amazing. If you are facing adversity however, love poems likely will just annoy you.

In "Poetry from my Heart", I attempted to divide the poems into categories which will fit your mood no matter what you are experiencing at the time you choose to explore them. There should be something for everyone, no matter whether you are

in love, out of love, you hurt, you are lonely, angry, abandoned, or you are facing other challenges in your life.

Poetry has a healing power that nurtures the soul and quietens the mind and so I hope that whatever your situation is in life, you found something here that helped you safely on your own journey.

Just a final word. Those who know me, will ask why I chose to publish this book under the name Paul Guerin. The answer is simple. It is to honour my Irish heritage and the name I was known by in Ireland as a young boy. It takes me right back to my roots.

Warm wishes

Paul Guerin

Made in the USA
Las Vegas, NV
21 May 2023